WHO WOULD WIN?

COYOTE

VS.

DINGO

BY
JERRY PALLOTTA

ILLUSTRATED BY
ROB BOLSTER

Scholastic Inc.

The publisher would like to thank the following for their kind permission to use their photographs in this book: Photos ©: 10 top: tobkatrina/Getty Images; 10 bottom: tommy_martin/Getty Images; 11 top: Africa Studio/Shutterstock.com; 12 top: nater23/Getty Images; 13 top: taviphoto/Getty Images; 17 bottom: Courtesy the Perth Mint; 18 top: johnaudrey/Getty Images; 25 top: Deliris/Shutterstock.com.

Welcome to the world, Reese Miller.
—*J. P.*

To all dog lovers.
—*R.B.*

Text copyright © 2023 by Jerry Pallotta.
Illustrations copyright © 2023 by Rob Bolster.

Library of Congress Cataloging-in-Publication Data available.
ISBN 978-1-338-67218-3

10 9 8 7 6 5 4 3 2 1   23 24 25 26 27

Printed in the U.S.A.
First printing, 2023

What would happen if a coyote and a dingo met each other? What if they were both hungry? What if they had a fight? Which one do you think would win?

MEET THE COYOTE

Scientific name: *Canis latrans*
A coyote is a four-legged mammal that looks like a dog.
It is a dog! Or is it a wolf? The truth is—it's both!

NAME ORIGIN
*The Aztec people named
it* coyotl, *which eventually
became* coyote.

OTHER NAMES
Brush wolf, prairie wolf, and American jackal

Dogs, coyotes, jackals, wolves, and foxes look similar
from afar. Coyotes are famous for their howl.
AAAAHHHH! Ooooooohhhh.

AAAAHHHHOooooohhhh

dog   coyote   jackal

MEET THE DINGO

Scientific name: *Canis dingo*

The dingo is known as the apex predator from Down Under. It is the largest land predator in Australia.

NAME ORIGIN
The Aboriginal people of Australia named the dingo.

SLANG
"Down Under" is slang for the continent of Australia.

Dingoes are similar to dogs, coyotes, jackals, wolves, and foxes. Animals in this group are called canines.

dingo   wolf   fox

NORTH AMERICA

The coyote is from North America. Coyotes are very adaptable. They live in all types of environments: forests, savannas, prairies, brush, deserts, mountains, farmlands, suburbs, and even big cities.

World

North America

North America

Atlantic Ocean

Pacific Ocean

South America

LEGEND

An explorer upon meeting his first coyote said, "It is smart like a fox, shaped like a dog, and ferocious like a wolf."

AUSTRALIA

The dingo is from Australia. The dingo lives in a tough and rugged environment. Australia has a mostly hot and dry climate.

Map

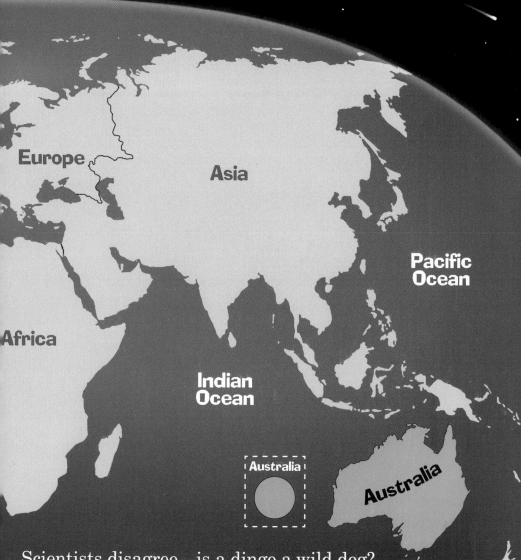

Scientists disagree—is a dingo a wild dog? Or is it more of a wolf?

SIZE

Here is a coyote next to a mastiff, the heaviest dog on earth. Coyotes are small. They are not as big as their reputations. They weigh about 35 pounds.

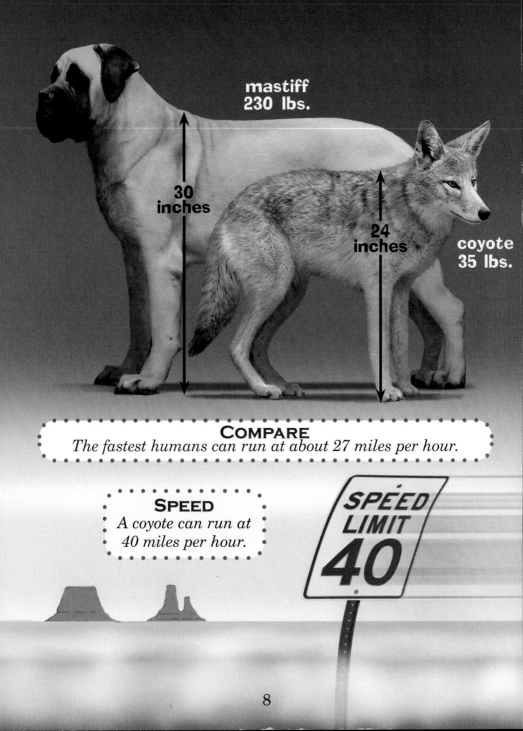

mastiff
230 lbs.

30 inches

24 inches

coyote
35 lbs.

COMPARE
The fastest humans can run at about 27 miles per hour.

SPEED
A coyote can run at 40 miles per hour.

SPEED LIMIT 40

SIZE

Here is a dingo next to an Irish wolfhound, the tallest dog on earth.

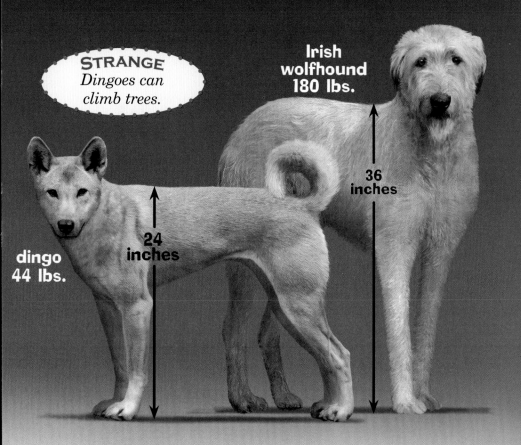

STRANGE
Dingoes can climb trees.

Irish wolfhound 180 lbs.

36 inches

24 inches

dingo 44 lbs.

SPEED
A dingo can run about 37 miles per hour. That's faster than a human.

SPEED LIMIT 37

DESCRIBE

Not many wild animals are trained to be pets. The dog is the most domesticated pet on earth. It is often called man's best friend. It is a woman's best friend, too!

DEFINITION
To be domesticated *means to become a pet or live on a farm. Some animals will never be pets.*

This border collie, a farm dog, is protecting a herd of sheep.

DID YOU KNOW?
Wild plants can also be domesticated into food and farmed.

10

A DOG

Dogs and other canines can be taught tasks and tricks. Dogs do not live as long as most mammals.

FACT
Many people use service dogs, also called seeing eye dogs or guide dogs.

AGING FACT
One dog year is equal to about 7 human years.

DID YOU KNOW?
Dogs sweat from their paws.

HAIR OR FUR?

Mammals have fur or hair. Some have long hair or fur. A coyote has short hair.

coyote hair

Here is a dog with long hair.

GROOMING FACT
Coyotes are usually scruffy-looking.

DID YOU KNOW?
Some dog owners bring their dogs to a dog hairdresser.

Afghan hound

HAIR OR FUR?

A dingo also has short hair.

dingo hair

OTHER NAME
A dingo is also called a warrigal.

Here is another dog with long hair!

komondor

POPULAR DOG

Here are some popular dog breeds.

Pekingese

terrier

Dalmatian

Chihuahua

DOG NAMES
Pooch, canine, hound

collie

Cavalier

bulldog

chow chow

dachshund

shepherd

BREEDS

Here are more, including some strange dog breeds.

pointer

corgi

Pomeranian

sharp-pei

Maltese

FUNNY NAMES
*Labradoodle,
goldendoodle*

Rottweiler

schnauzer

husky

setter

shih-tzu

SKELETON

This is a coyote skeleton. It looks exactly like a typical mammal. It has a head, neck, body, ribs, and four legs. It also has a tail.

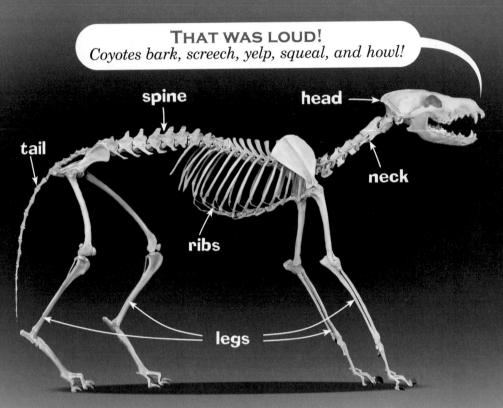

THAT WAS LOUD!
Coyotes bark, screech, yelp, squeal, and howl!

spine

head

tail

neck

ribs

legs

LIGAMENTS VS. TENDONS

Ligaments connect bone to bone. Tendons connect bone to muscle. Cartilage covers the ends of bones, acting like padding.

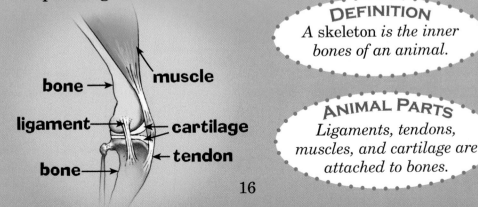

bone →

← muscle

ligament →

← cartilage

← tendon

bone →

DEFINITION
A skeleton *is the inner bones of an animal.*

ANIMAL PARTS
Ligaments, tendons, muscles, and cartilage are attached to bones.

16

SKELETON

This is what a dingo skeleton looks like. It is very similar to a coyote skeleton. A dingo can turn its head 180 degrees around. It can stand straight and look behind.

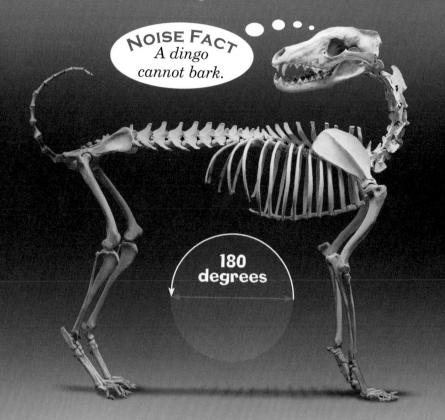

NOISE FACT
A dingo cannot bark.

180 degrees

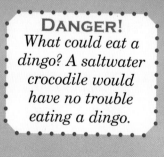

DANGER!
What could eat a dingo? A saltwater crocodile would have no trouble eating a dingo.

MONEY FACT
Australia has a dingo coin.

Australian 2 oz. Dingo Silver Coin

TEETH

Notice the teeth in a coyote skull. Coyotes and other canines have meat-eating carnivore-type teeth. Their teeth are designed to hold animals, then crack bones and cut meat and tendons.

holders

bone cracking

meat and tendon cutters

TAIL DOWN

A coyote has a bushy tail. When it runs, its tail is down, not out straight like most dogs.

SKULL

This is a dingo skull.

PARTS OF THE SKULL

upper jaw

canine
teeth

lower jaw

carnassial
teeth

TAIL UP

The dingo tail is bushy. The tail is up flying in the breeze
when the dingo is running.

DNA FACT
*Scientists have learned that
the dingo is related to the New
Guinea singing dog.*

FOOD

It was thought that coyotes killed cattle, hogs, and other big farm animals.

horse

cow

sheep

pig

donkey

goat

We now know that coyotes mostly eat small animals like rats, mice, and rabbits.

rat

mouse

rabbit

PACK FACT
Coyotes do not hunt in packs

FOOD

Dingoes are the apex mammal predator in Australia. Watch out, wallabies, bunnies, koalas, bandicoots, numbats, and quolls. A dingo will eat you! If you are a big kangaroo or wallaroo, a pack of dingoes will eat you.

APEX FACT
Apex *means "top of the food chain."*

GROUP FACT
Dingoes do hunt in packs.

FOOD FACT
Dingoes also eat reptiles, fish, and birds.

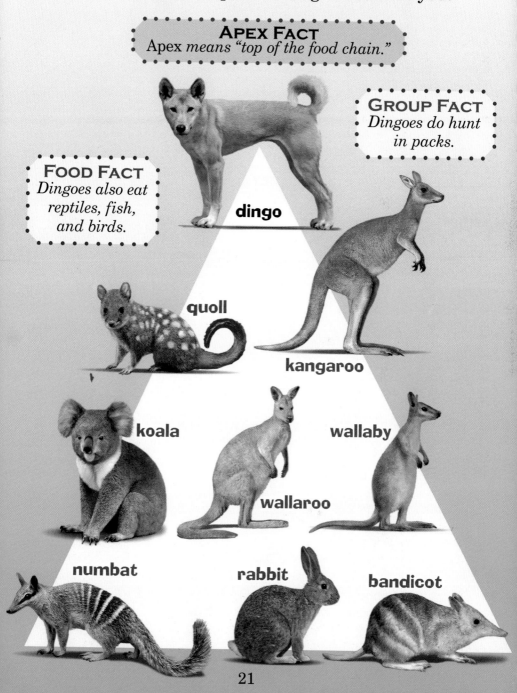

dingo

quoll

kangaroo

koala

wallaby

wallaroo

numbat

rabbit

bandicot

PAWS

This is a coyote footprint. This is a coyote paw. The big print behind the toes is the foot pad.

FOOTPRINT TOE COUNT

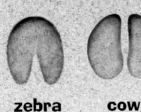   

zebra	cow	sloth	hippo	elephant
1	2	3	4	5

FOOTPRINTS

This is a dingo paw. This is a dingo footprint. Four toes in front, and a foot pad.

FOOTPRINT TOE COUNT

horse	giraffe	rhino	tapir	readers of this book
1	2	3	4	5

UGLY HISTORY

It is not the coyote's fault, but they have an ugly history. They used to live only out in the western area of North America. Coyotes got blamed by ranchers for missing livestock and poultry.

DEFINITION
Livestock *is cattle, cows, horses, pigs, and goats.*

GOVERNMENT POLICY
The US federal and state governments have been killing coyotes by shooting, poisoning, and trapping. Instead of being wiped out, coyotes are more numerous than ever.

The demise of wolves allowed coyotes to move east into big cities, such as Boston, New York, Philadelphia, Chicago, Atlanta, and Pittsburgh.

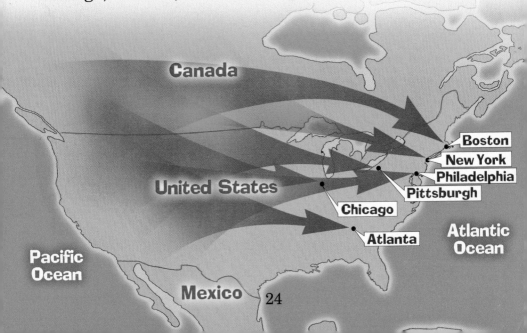

Canada

Boston
New York
Philadelphia
Pittsburgh

United States

Chicago

Atlanta

Atlantic Ocean

Pacific Ocean

Mexico

MISUNDERSTOOD

In Australia, dingoes were accused of killing thousands of sheep. They were also accused of killing cattle.

The government of Australia has tried to wipe out the dingo. They even built a 3,000-mile fence. There are dingoes on one side, and no dingoes on the other side.

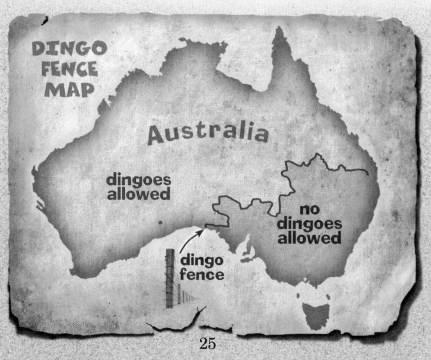

DINGO FENCE MAP

Australia

dingoes allowed

no dingoes allowed

dingo fence

SNEAKY

WHO TOOK THE FUNNY PAGES?

A coyote was seen riding a train in Portland, Oregon.

CRASH!

A coyote got hit by a car but then hitched a ride 20 miles inside the grill and bumper.

ALL ABOARD!

Coyotes have jumped rides on moving trains.

REPUTATION

LINGO
The way different animals talk. Here's some dingo sign language!

BINGO
A number matching game.

RINGO
A dingo drumming.

It is time for the fight! The coyote tries to trick the dingo. It enters a hollow log and throws up. The smell attracts the dingo to battle but the coyote left the area and is hiding in some bushes.

The dingo is not happy. He goes looking for the coyote.

The coyote then sneaks back and hides in the log. The dingo does not see him. Where is that coyote? Come out and fight! After a while, the dingo follows the scent.

He is now face-to-face with the coyote. The coyote outsmarted himself. He is stuck in the log. He can't back up. The coyote has to confront the dingo.

The coyote can't escape. The dingo opens his mouth and bites the coyote in the jaw. Crunch! Ouch!

The coyote has a cut tongue, sore mouth, and broken teeth—he can't fight back. The dingo blocks the opening.

The dingo gives the coyote a few more bites. The ferocious dingo wins and walks away.

WHO HAS THE ADVANTAGE? CHECKLIST

COYOTE		DINGO
☐	Size	☐
☐	Speed	☐
☐	Eyesight	☐
☐	Fur	☐
☐	Paws	☐
☐	Teeth	☐

This is one way the fight might have ended. How would you write the ending?